THE

SNOW

WAS

FALLING

THE

SNOW

WAS

FALLING

Volume VIII
2014

Arthur R. Marinello

PREFACE

My bent seems to be reviewing the past and that bent seems to pervade other subjects as well. All well and good. I must go with the flow.

This volume was done, all of it, written in one year. I have little influence on the matter.

A.R.M.
November 27, 2015

TABLE OF CONTENTS

A POUND OF PASTA

10:30 am, Saturday
March 15, 2014

I was just reading
An article on the
New Maserati,
An upscale car,
Selling for many thousands

And then talking
With my daughter
About such
And also about
Houses
Costing millions

And that many
People
Go for these things,
So expensive,
And undoubtedly
Delight in them

And I find it incomprehensible

Some of us have
A minimalist
Tendency

A pound of pasta costs little.

PUTIN

7:55 am, Tuesday
March 18, 2014

Putin
Putin, the Russian dictator
Proud for his country
And ambitious

Faces a complex world

He must pretend
To be democratic,
Though neither he
Nor his countrymen
Believe in such

And he must get back
His country's
Former lands
Whilst pretending

It is glory he seeks
Dangers would not restrain him
Or suffering
Only his conscience

Certainly not sanctions

DECISIONS

8:02 am, Tuesday
March 18, 2014

Decisions
Decisions, decisions

Always an important factor
In life
And major

Consciously
And unconsciously
They are made

And as one becomes older
And still they
Must be made
There are incursions
Others feel they must
Make decisions for you
Without the facts
The feelings
The perspective
That you have

Nor the authority

THE SNOW WAS FALLING

3:15 pm, Saturday
March 29, 2014

I was just now
Sitting on my patio
A small place

And I was thinking
Of various things

My parents certainly
And how I don't
Hear from them

My father passed,
As they say,
Before the war
And my mother after

When the memory
Came to me
Of a time
When I was given
A pass to go to Brussels

And Captain Simon
Commanding Officer
Of the intelligence team
Paired with mine

Asked me to deliver
A personal note
To a woman
In a nightclub there

Which I did

On the two or three days
That I was in Brussels
I attended the opera
And saw *La Boheme*

It was on the way back
From the opera
Toward my hotel
That I walked
This street
A main street
I suppose
That I saw this
Unbelievable scene

Stretched out for
The whole length
Of the street were
Belgian girls or young ladies

They were standing
Shoulder to shoulder
Five or six deep
Waiting in the night
For someone
Anyone
Who would have them

On my return to my outfit
I found that they had
The Nineteenth Corps,
That is,
Crossed the Rhine River
In my absence

It must have been
In the ensuing nights
That the Germans
Shelled us throughout the night
As we slept on the ground
And snow was falling

THE LAWS

7:55 am, Saturday
April 5, 2014

Last evening
We were, my wife and I,
Watching a report
From Afghanistan
On the abuse of women

Some of them, that is,
Who ran afoul
Of their laws
Or their customs

Some were beaten
Some tortured
Some murdered

All this because of
A strange or not so strange
Juxtaposition of laws

There is Islamic law
And tribal law
Very strict
Quite punitive

There is the law of
A democracy
International law too
And human law

Constitutional law
 And others

And people get caught
In the crossfire
A brutal matter

There is the law
Of the savage

Or the law of reality

Twelve years ago
New York's Twin Towers
Were bombed, destroyed

Over three thousand died
And others were added

Ten or twenty or more
Were the perpetrators

And then the laws
Of insanity
Of imbecility came into play

In an effort
Or supposed effort
To punish the perpetrators,
Wars were unleashed

Which, while it may have
Profited the arms dealers
And others,
Resulted in the deaths
Of hundreds of thousands

Actually, those hundreds
Of thousands
We might well presume
Were innocent

A strange mathematics
Of the Insane
Of the imbecilic
Had prevailed

MOST WOMEN

12:50 pm, Sunday
April 13, 2014

Most women are beautiful
Despite what they think
They're beautiful

The extra efforts
Made to make them
Beautiful
Are misleading
They already are

I don't think
That God would
Venture on the scene
With any other plan in mind

So there you have it
They're beautiful

But that's just
The beginning
There's more

They're placed in roles
That are indispensable

Take for instance
Their attracting men
Or a man
And ensuring the survival
Of the race

The stability of this
Human experience

The nurturing
The idealism
The inspiration
There is currently
The abuse of women
Of girls even

In places like Afghanistan
In India
In the various countries
Of Africa

And by many different means
In our own countries as well

And there is, also,
The misguiding
By leaders
Especially by politicians

Our leaders
Our politicians
Could be forgiven on the grounds
That they have no clue

They are so idiotic
And so focused on
Their own careers
Their salaries
Their images
Their security
And so driven by their fears
Their lack of courage

And so laughable
If it weren't so tragic
Some hope to do well by women
By making them more like men

I've known a number
Of good men
Not many

But I've known a lot more
Good women

Men are superior to women
In some ways

But women easily
Leave them in the dust
They are so superior

God made man
And woman

Do you think He was
Fooling around?

JOSEPHINE

7:25 pm, Sunday
April 13, 2014

My mother was an immigrant
From Naples

She was nineteen years old

She arrived with her mother
Filomena
On the San Giorgio
The date was July 12, 1912

It is possible that she
Was not an immigrant
But a tourist

She nevertheless remained
Having met and married
The man who was to
Become my father

She bore him six children
The two females
My sisters
Did not long survive

Thus, my mother
Knew tragedy and heartache

Danger she had experienced too
It was she, no doubt,
Who told me
Of running in panic
From the lava coming
From Mount Vesuvius
Through the streets
Of Naples

She lived a short life
Dying at fifty-two
In nineteen forty-six

She lived the terrors
Of a mother
Whose sons
Were in the war
Terrors which wore her down
Adding to the
Sudden and tragic
Death of my father
After twenty-two years
Of marriage

They lived in Manhattan
Then New Jersey
Then Brooklyn

This may all seem
Pretty grim
As surely it was

But when I think
Of my mother
I don't get a sense
Of such

And understandably so

The sense
The picture
I have of my mother
Is of a flesh and blood
Woman
Always on the side of hope
Of survival
Of joy
Of a Neapolitan
Energy
Calmness
Faith

She was not, however,
Indestructible
And with the war
And other stresses
And having to face them
Alone
It was no contest

She remains for me,
However,
The model of womanhood
A model of the human

I have never met a person
Who matches
Her sense of love
Of devotion
Of sacrifice

And, also,
Honesty
Intelligence
Steadfastness

You get the picture

WE'VE GOT TO LOOK

6:05 pm, Wednesday
April 16, 2014

We've got to look
Beyond ourselves
And see others
The other person

We've got to acknowledge
The other person's
Existence

We need not focus so much
On ourselves

We, each of us,
Has a tendency
To take care
Of ourselves
Anyway

What has merit
Is
To consider
The other person

SUCH A PLEASURE

6:08 pm, Wednesday
April 16, 2014

It's such a pleasure
To go outside
To sit outside

To have the contact
With the world
Outside

The freedom of it
The communing
With Nature

The freedom from
The limitations inside

Yes
A pleasure

MIRACLES

7:03 pm, Holy Thursday
April 17, 2014

Miracles
Miracles
What can I say about miracles?

The other day a woman said
In the papers, it was reported,
That Jesus Christ
Was a fake

Well, that's nice
It's always good
To be informed

So, now what do we do
About miracles?

It's worse than that
The miracles that I know of
Or think I know of
Happened in church
Or are church-related

So that
If Christ is a fake
Someone else is involved

And so,
What shall we call him
Or her?

Admittedly
It's not easy to believe
In miracles
Or in Christ

It takes what is called
Faith

I don't know
What to do about it

GOOD FRIDAY

11:30 am, Good Friday
April 18, 2014

I am sitting down
To write this
In a state of
Quasi-exhaustion

Today is Good Friday
And Easter Sunday is
Close at hand
My wife had asked me
To bake some Challah

Challah is an egg bread
Favored by Jewish people
In fact, the recipe I use
Came, originally,
From the Jewish mother
Of a convert monk
And was found in a book
Written by a fellow Jesuit

Anyway,
My wife went shopping
And I thought I would
Surprise her and prepare
The dough
While she was gone

It did turn out to be
A surprise
Certainly for me

I put all the ingredients out
Flour, water, yeast, egg,
Et cetera

And I began to assemble
Using the Cuisinart
Which is a mystery to me
And I was done,
I thought

Not so
As I turned around
I noticed that I'd forgotten
The egg

I did my best to mix
The egg in
And I took the dough
And put it on the board
To knead
When I noticed that
I'd forgotten the yeast
And so I then added that

Now, this may sound simple
But it isn't

You can't do things this way

And now I'm wondering
If the dough will rise

My wife has mercifully
Arrived
And she laughed

LOBELIA

11:12 am, Holy Saturday
April 19, 2014

In today's paper
In the garden section
There was something
On Lobelia
And not for the first time,
I was amazed to read
That there are 415
Varieties
Of Lobelia

How come this plentitude
Of varieties

And then,
Some ten or twenty years ago
As an amateur woodworker
I became aware
While working with Mahogany
That there were something
Like 500 varieties
Of Mahogany trees

Again, . . . how come?

I think we currently have
Seven billion people
On this earth
Up from only
Hundreds or thousands
Or millions
In earlier times

Not too far back
It was felt that there was
The Earth, little more

And now we've become aware
Of many planets
Planets called stars
Stars called planets

It seems we have
Multiple universes
Galaxies
Whatever you call such

And so, there are hundreds
Perhaps thousands of planets

Wherefore?

JUST KIDS

4:55 pm, Wednesday
April 23, 2014

On my walk this morning
Someone called my name
He was across the street
And when I couldn't
Recognize him
He came across the street
And was soon followed
By a couple whom
I did know

And the four of us
Talked

About a number of things
Mostly about adventures
In the war
Mine

But something struck me
Strikes me

The original person
Told of a recent happening

A man had shot
Two intruders
Who had broken a window
Through which they crawled

He killed them
Apparently justified
In the eyes of the
Teller of the story
They had violated
The sanctity of his home
And he had been prepared

The intruders were
Sixteen and eighteen
Just kids

I WON'T MENTION

7:05 pm, Sunday
April 27, 2014

I won't mention
Any names
But I've come to realize
That some people will enter
Your home
And not know how
To behave

I wish I could say
It's the younger
Or youngest generation
But I'm afraid not

By reason of family
Or friendship
They are permitted
So to behave

It's probably a form
Of bullying
Resulting in a form of disruption
Or unease
How sad

THE BILLIONAIRE

9:55 am, Thursday
May 1, 2014

The other day
There were two items
In the papers

One showed people
Mothers and children
Marching, sort of,
To raise awareness
And to protest
Prostitution activity
On their streets
Or nearby
Seeking to rescue
Girls and women
And to incarcerate
Their managers, boyfriends,
Commonly known as pimps

The other news item
Involved a billionaire
Owner of a basketball team
Married
But primarily with a girlfriend

Who had made
Not very commendable reference
To Negroes
Currently referred to
As blacks

And I was thinking of
Relationships

Now relationships,
I believe,
Are not only important
Not only vital
But, it seems,
Are what we're here for

Relationships are the avenue
Through which a human being
Expresses love
Which is also what
We're here for

Now, this is not
Always
Done . . . expressed
As we would like

Even in marriage
A primary vehicle
For this super-important
Thing
Called love

Or in families

Not to mention businesses
Or in any searching, grasping
For money
Or glory
Or whatever

And so, getting back
To these people
Referred to as prostitutes
Though I prefer to see them
As immensely mistreated
By fate

And their being exhorted
By people whose relationships
Are likely pretty solid
To give up the only relationship
They have
And get on with their lives

And this billionaire
Whose relationships
Whose ability to form
Relationships is faulty
Except, perhaps, to money

I can see putting that money
Which obviously has not
Helped him
To some use
Helping the afore-mentioned
Unlucky ones

Say, ten or twenty or more
Thousands
Applied to each
Fractured relationship type
Enabling the journey
To relationships
More ideal
And enabling the billionaire
To express a life-giving
Humanness

Both sides of the equation

FAULTS OF MY OWN

7:50 am, Thursday
May 8, 2014

I don't want to
Mention any names

But it seems
To me
That some people
Have a negative twist
On things

You might say
Something

And the rejoinder
Unasked for
Is negative
Or somewhat so

I might go further
And say
That a negative bent
May pertain
More to some cultures
Than to others

I think I've experienced
Such

Just think about it

I've been exposed
To a number of different cultures
Enough of each
To see a pattern

One such is predictably
Cynical

Another blatantly
Materialistic

And so on

I cannot claim to be
Without faults
Of my own

Surely, I've been accused
Of such

INSTINCT

8:02 am, Thursday
May 8, 2014

There are some women
Young women
Who feel that women
Are different
From men

Now what to make of this

Our culture trumpets
Something somewhat
Different

On the larger stage
Women who compete
Successfully
In a man's world,
As they say,
Are lauded
Greatly so

Even in schools
Meant to be
Places of learning
Such seems to be the case

Do you think it must
Require a concerted effort
On the part of females
To realize otherwise?

Otherwise than
What they're taught?

Really
I think not

I think that
There's always
That God-given
Sense

That instinct

Which tells them otherwise

THE CHINESE

9:00 am, Monday
May 19, 2014

No one likes to be shamed
But look at this

On the news this morning
A lot of time was given
To the hacking
On the part of the Chinese

Actually, an arm of
Their government

Of American secrets
Of American corporations
Of the ingenuity
Of Americans

And the Americans
Are suing the Chinese
Accusing the Chinese
Of criminal activity

Which, in fact, causes
Much unemployment
In this country
And the Americans

Are asking
For the Chinese
To admit their transgression
And cease

And, this may work,
And it may not

But I began to think
That a different tactic
Might work
If the first one fails

That the Chinese
Might be urged
To reconsider
Their nefarious activities
Which seem to imply
That the Chinese
Are being told that they lack
Intelligence
Creativity
And resort to activities
Which denigrate their self-worth

SOME EXPERIENCES

12:45 pm, Saturday
May 2, 2014

Some experiences seem
To last
A lifetime

Here in California in 2014
Came to me
As I was having lunch
With my wife
An evening in Camp Dix
In 1938

I was in the ring, somehow,
And when my name
Was announced
Someone in the audience
Of some 2,000 young soldiers
Yelled out
"Marinello, you're a bum"

And then in 1 minute and 15 seconds
I knocked out my opponent
 To my eternal shame
 And regret

GEORGIE PATTON

9:00 am, Monday
Memorial Day
May 26, 2014

The other day
My wife made mention
Of an incident
In the Second World War
That I'd experienced

I had delivered
Or was in the process
Of delivering
Some maps or something
On the presence of enemy soldiers
Or emplacements

We were still in Normandy
It would have been
Before the Battle of St. Lo

It was in the dark of
The evening
All in blackout
And I entered the tent
Of the G-2
The intelligence headquarters
Of the XX Corps

And, as I entered
The G-2, a colonel
Barked at me,
"What's that on your face
Lieutenant?"

I was a bit stunned
Or something
I didn't know for sure
What he meant
I had a moustache
And had lately grown
A Van Dyke beard

When he said for me
To get rid of such
And that the general
That is the very famous
General George Patton

Would be at my outfit
The next morning

My wife thought that
General Patton himself
Had upbraided me

No, the colonel
Had done the threatening

Well, Patton did not
Show up
The next day

But, too late,
I had shaved off
Both moustache and beard

And it was many years later
That I resurrected
The moustache

PERIPATETICS

2:05 pm, Thursday
June 5, 2014

A few hours ago
My wife said that
Every time she uses the
Glasses on the upper shelf
Of the cupboard
She thinks of Whip

Whip was an older man
I had met many years ago
On the mile walk
I used to take
Daily

Eventually,
When my wife
Retired from teaching
And we'd walk together
We also met
Irene, his wife,
And, almost regularly,
We'd stop by and visit
In their front porch

And we'd talk
And became good
Really close friends

They were of German descent
I think
Their name was Stahl
From Nebraska, I think,
And after some sixty years
In California
They returned to Nebraska
Where, some few years later,
 They died

In my early walks
I also met
Fateh, a Hindu from India,
And we'd have conversations
His wife was totally invalided
And, in the evenings,
He would take her out for walks
In a wheelchair

Fateh had been a police chief
In Northern India
And when his wife died
And we went to their
Temple services

And she was cremated
As was their custom
I was somewhat disturbed
It was my first such experience

Walks, then,
Can be quite broadening

Now that my walks
Are shorter
I still get involved

Also, we've become friends
With Fateh's daughter
And son-in-law
Who is a cardiologist

And when we eat together
We don't eat meat
Such is their custom

And the Stahls
They'd offer us whiskey
In the morning

And there are others

Many Armenians have
Moved into our
Neighborhood

And we have Thais
And Mexicans

And so we have
This community
Like a small town
A little bit of this
Huge city

A community
Of the peripatetics

MACULAR DEGENERATION

11:20 am, Wednesday
June 11, 2014

There is a condition
Of the eyes
Called macular degeneration
Which leads to blindness

I've been in treatment
For this condition
For almost two years
For one eye
And now for both

It involves an injection
At the base of
The eyeball

To me it's quite
Traumatic
It is the worst
Physical and psychological
Assault
I've ever experienced

This morning I was talking
To an elderly client

A few months ago
She was in such anxiety
That for a few months
She was practically immobilized

As we were talking
And she informed me
Of various things currently
In her life
She mentioned an upcoming
Driver's test
Which she had failed
At least twice

And, she said,
"I'm not going to
Worry about it"

And, in my morning walk
I wondered,

"Could I do that?"

EACH LIFE

4:19 pm, Friday
June 13, 2014

As we go through life
Trying as best we can
To deal with life's realities
Avoiding pitfalls
Providing for ourselves
And for those
Entrusted to our care

We must, most importantly,
Cherish each life
That comes our way

Our lives are centered,
As they say,
Our focus is secure
Not to worry
Our attention
Our thoughts
Our efforts
Must be on others

Each life we encounter
Must be treated gently
Handled with care

MOM, POP

7:46 pm, Saturday
June 14, 2014

Mom, Pop,
Where are you?

It's been so long
And I haven't heard

You had such a marriage
It must have been so
Special
As the two of you
Started out

Special people
Yes, there were upsets
Many

But I was nearby
When the two of you
Discussed things

I could tell
You were a team

A couple of real humans

THE ROCK

9:55 am, Thursday
June 19, 2014

There are leaves
That move
And rivers

But a rock
Doesn't

A rock is still
It endures
More or less

And, as others
Let themselves go
Wherever, however,
Expressing
Emoting
Being irresponsible
Recognizing
No restrictions
A rock
Remains
Still
Reliable . . . for others

TRAITS

7:30 am, Thursday
June 26, 2014

Let's say
We, each of us,
Has seventy traits

And the degree
Or extent of each
Is different
For each of us

And these traits
Are mingled
In each
Succeeding progeny

And that the extent
Of the differences
In each
Is limitless,
You might say

You might say that a trait
Here and there
Becomes almost
Unrecognizable

Let's take casualness
In the generation
Being considered
It may actually be
Harmless

But in the next
It could be calamitous
With critical matters
Being practically ignored

Or pride,
Intelligence
Fear
Envy
Deviousness
And so on

That's not all
Suppose we had
Each of us
One hundred and seventy-five
Traits

MASS

8:47 am, Thursday
June 20, 2014

It's nice
To go to Mass

Some thirty-five years ago,
My wife and I
Went to daily Mass
At 6:30 am

And each time,
Mysteriously,
I would get something
Out of it

From the readings
Or the homily
Or something

And some spot in me
Unknowingly vacant
Was filled

And this went on for
The five years
We did this

And I would like
To resume the practice now
But I'm too old,
Really

PAVANE

5:10 pm, Thursday
July 3, 2014

How can you not know
Ravel's
*Pavane pour une enfante
Defunte*?

There are others
But really
This pavane
Does grab your attention

But, as I say,
There are others

How can you fail
To know
That there is
Music,
Real music?

And there is so much of it

COMMUNICATION WITH THE PAST

5:05 pm, Wednesday
July 16, 2014

Yesterday,
I went in for
Eye surgery
For macular degeneration

An unpleasant experience
To say the least

And, I don't remember
How it came about,
But come about it did

Could this condition
Have a genetic
A hereditary component
To it?

And, yes, it might

I have a paper
Something written
Like a scrawl
All over the page

A writing by a
Great aunt

This was a person
I'd never met

A nun

And she had gone blind

She was my Sicilian grandmother's
Sister

But, that's not all

A month or so ago
As a result of a
Conversation
With my friend, Vince,
Also Sicilian
Or of Sicilian origin,

Same hometown,

He graciously offered
To do some searching
Of family
In the past

He confirmed
Something I'd heard
Somehow, somewhere,

That I'd had
A great uncle
Who was a priest

This, as he — Vince, that is —
Found record of my
Grandparents' marriage

And that the officiating priest
Was my great-uncle,
Rosolino

So, there you have it
Communicating with the past

SALVATORE

4:49 pm, Wednesday
July 23, 2014

My father
Was a linotype operator
No . . . not really

He was much more
Than that

 In fact, just looking
At linotyping alone
He apparently was . . .
The backbone
Of the operation
Judging from a card
Written to him by a colleague
When he was away
For a while
Undergoing surgery

Yes, he was a backbone
Type of person
Certainly, amongst
His relatives, his cousins

And we could learn
Something from that
Which is that
As a leader
When you need support
It may not be forthcoming

Anyway, getting back to
Linotyping,
One Saturday morning
My father took me
To his place of work
In Manhattan
Fremont-Payne
Printer of law books

And he showed me the procedure
Whereby those books were set up

Lead was heated to
A molten state
And poured into
Receptacles
Each being a letter
And, after solidifying,
Would enable the printing

Such a procedure no longer
Exists
It was tragically
Destructive
And,
In the end,
It did him in

He arrived in America
In 1903
Along with his father,
Mother, sister, and brother
On board the *California*

They left from Palermo
The ancestral home was in
Cinisi
Where I visited
Seventy-four years later
And saw the house where
They had lived
My cousins there
Pointed it out to me

Growing up I had a father
Who was, in many ways,
Unique

He lived in two worlds,
Basically,
Or more than two

He was in an immigrant world
A world his cousins inhabited

And there were many of them

But, unlike his cousins,
He was very much a part
Of an American world
New York City . . . Manhattan
And the Metropolitan Opera
Encompassed both

Opera was one of his passions
He heard . . . he saw
The great . . . the stars of his time
Caruso, Gigli, Ponselle,
And all the rest

He would sing the great arias
In subdued or sotto voce

One of his hobbies was book binding

Some marriages
Are love marriages
His surely was
My mother and he
Were a team
A team of individuals
Six children

But some things in this life
Turn out to be insurmountable
The true nature of some
Successes unknown
Until too late

And so we lost our anchor,
Father and husband,

And learned early
Of the hardness of life
And that life's tragedies
Are meant to be overcome
Must be overcome

LIFE IS

Life is made up of
Decisions
Good and bad
We make them

Life is made up of
Attitudes
The same

And, surely, life is
A happenstance
Kind of thing

But those decisions we make
Hardly ever knowing
Their import
Till afterwards

And courage is an
Attitude
And honesty
And dishonesty
And love

Always love

EDDIE

8:14 am, Tuesday
July 29, 2014

My brother is
Ninety years old
Today

My baby brother
My kid brother

We were all of us
Born in Manhattan
In my mother's bed

My kid brother is now
Living in Long Island
Much closer to our
Origins than the rest of us

We were in the war together
The Second World War

In some of the same
Battles
Or campaigns

The Battle for Normandy
The Battle of the Bulge

Comrades in arms
We were

Eddie in Mainz on Rhine in 1945

The author and his brother, Eddie,
taken in Regensburg, Germany in June 1945

THE HERB PICKERS

8:28 am, Tuesday
July 29, 2014

As I was entering
My library
An hour or so ago
My wife was entering
From the garden

Her hands holding
A batch of herbs
For this morning's breakfast
Tuesday
Egg Tuesday

"My herb picker is not
Picking," she said

True enough
The pains and frailties
Of old age
Impinge themselves
On one's capabilities

And on those herbs
Thyme, Oregano, Chives,
Basil, Rosemary

SAINTS

8:32 am, Tuesday
July 29, 2014

When you think about it,
It's such a privilege
To be on this earth
While saints are
Among us

It's easy to say
Mother Theresa
Is here
Was here

But that doesn't
Tell the story

There are saints
Really,
Saints

They are here
Among us

They're all around us

SICILIANS

6:30 pm, Thursday
August 7, 2014

I was thinking
Just a while ago
Of a time way back
1945, I think

The war was winding down
In Germany
And I was visiting
I'm not sure what

But . . . here I was
In a prisoner-of-war camp
The POWs were Italian
Their leader, I was told,
Was a major
But he never showed up

I was surrounded by
These Italian prisoners
Ten or twenty of them
Pleased to have this American
Of Italian descent
Among them

When, suddenly, this corporal
Begged me
To please say a few words
To him
In Sicilian

Having found that I was
Of Sicilian descent
Because, he said,
He missed it so much
Amongst his fellow prisoners

Sicilians dancing in So. California

UNCLE TONY

12:45 pm, Thursday
August 28, 2014

My uncle was an epileptic
Which meant
Among other things
That I witnessed a number
Of grand mal seizures
Early in life

To say that he was
An epileptic
Is misleading
For he was a gentle soul
Fond of the young ones
Around him

He was seven years old
When, with his family,
He came to America
And, probably, when
I was seven
I would have witnessed
A number of his seizures

I remember him best
When all of us lived
In Lyndhurst, New Jersey
He lived with his mother, a widow,
And when she left for Manhattan
Probably in 1928, he also left
With my grandmother

It was said that the cause
Of his condition
Was a fall from a horse
When he was four

In the early days
Of the twentieth century
The life of an epileptic
Was far different

I assume there were
No medications
Or special services

And I often have
Wondered
What became of him
I didn't see him again

A limited life
A gentle soul . . . a precious one

IT WAS THE SPIRIT

3:33 pm, Monday
September 8, 2014

I was sitting in my library
Just a minute ago
Looking at the many
Things I have done
I have built

The bookshelves
The desk
The chair

And all the other things
I have done

Yes, there's all this birch

The tile
And all that other stuff
Copious

And I began to see
To realize
What was behind it all

It was the spirit
The spirit was the whole thing

And there was more to it

There was marriage

I would not have done
So much
Without my wife
By my side

Or at least in the house
As much of the time
I was in the garage
In my workshop
With all those tools

There was the spirit
Yes
And behind it
Beside it
Was my wife

TEN MONTHS

9:44 am, Thursday
September 11, 2014

It all happened
In ten months

It started in May
My special month
The Germans surrendered

It was May of 1945
One or two days
Before my prediction

And we began
To settle down
In Bad Nauheim

And a pleasant month or so
Al Dennehy . . . Francine

And the atom bomb
On Japan
And another surrender
In early August

And off we were
We were going home

Sailing across the Atlantic
To Boston
New York dock workers
Were on strike

And arrival on October twelfth
To Brooklyn
To my mother
Frail and worn
Only fifty-two

Mustered out that January
A day before
My mother's death

And a bleak February
Brooklyn College
And Vera

That was it
Ten months

I'M REPORTING IT

11:00 am, Saturday
September 20, 2014

The spirit is
A fickle thing

I hate to say it
But it's true

For perhaps the
Hundredth time

I had an idea
To write something
A vivid something
Easy to remember
But postponed
Maybe an hour or so ago

But it's vanished

I have no idea

But it's true
I'm reporting it

LEFT BEHIND

1:10 pm, Sunday
October 12, 2014

I should say something
About this
About old age, that is

I fell on my brick patio
Two days ago
Old age it is

What to do about
This old age
That has been handed to us
Handed to us by
The increased awareness
That comes with what we call
The modern day
The various strategies

And we stumble along
And look at what once we did
And can do no longer

And see our friends
Stumble on for five or ten years
Till the end

It's not so bad
But we need perspective
This is all so new
So unexpected

Not many months ago
I could do gardening
And other chores
I no longer can
And I struggle to
Get it all back

What has happened to family
Which would soften the blow
Were it here?

Gone is the sweep
The surge
All part of the advance
To greater heights
Leaving us, inevitably,
Behind

THE SAINT MAKER

12:34 pm, Thursday
October 16, 2014

I was talking to
Father John
An hour or so ago

And I may have said
To him
Or thought of him
As a sort of saint maker

It was through him
Three or four years ago
That our small group
Provided his village
In Uganda
With its first well
And then a second
Perhaps a third

And so,
Completely, he described
The current state of affairs
In the village

Elimination of many diseases
A much healthier life
More food
Goats

I get a lot
Even primary credit
For the very special
Venture

But consider this

As he was one day
Telling us about his village
And the daily life
And boys getting water
In the early morning
My wife whispered to me
That we ought to do something

And I spoke up
And volunteered to build
A well
A magnificent thing
A miraculous thing
And it was Ray who
Sent us over the top

So, there you have it
My wife
And Ray
What do you think?

MARCHING

9:11 am, Friday
October 17, 2014

Just back from a visit to
The physical therapist
For help to improve
My balance
My strength
My everything

And one recommended
Exercise
Against a counter
To march in place

And I remarked
That everything
Reminds me of the Army
Or, at least, some things

The time I was maybe twenty
And our company
Returning from a long march
Many miles
Knapsacks
And as we, bedraggled,

Neared the end of the march
Were greeted with a band
Playing . . .
And we perked up

SONGS

10:20 am, Saturday
October 25, 2014

The songs my mother
Used to sing
Were Neapolitan
An aura of romance to them

Even "O Sole Mio"
Which is a paean to the sun

And there was
"Dicitincelle Vuio"
And "Torn a Surrienta"
Plaintive beauties

My father, on the other hand,
Would sing sotto voce
Arias from the opera

"E lucevan le stelle"
"Ridi Pagliaccio"

My mother's songs
Were of the morning
My father's
At other times
Yes, there were songs

EVIL

10:35 am, Saturday
October 25, 2014

Some ten or so years ago
I began to hear stories
Out of my hometown
Of Brooklyn, New York
And there about

Of Russian immigrant women
Or woman
Fainting upon entering
A supermarket
Overcome at the sight
Of all that plentitude

Today there is much mayhem
In places like Syria, Iraq
The killing of people
Of all ages

And some escape to
The U.S.
Where there is a somewhat
More peaceful life
And a plentitude
They had previously
Not known

In both locales
There exist, somewhat,
Human beings

Essentially the same
Or similar

Of course, there are differences

Catholics are said to believe
That the devil exists
Accounting for the evil

I'm not up to snuff
On the theology
Of all this

But evil exists
And it seems to be
Beyond us

What do you think?

ALL OVER YOU

1:35 pm, Sunday
November 2, 2014
All Souls Day

It's nice to be young
To be seven or eight
Or fifteen

To have a hat on, a coat
Or not
To have the snow
Falling on you
All over you

And, perhaps,
To be on a sled

It's nice to be
In a grammar school
Midst all that activity
That newness
The newness of life

And high school
To be in high school
Confronting that median stage
To adulthood
It's nice

And then, really
Adulthood
Work, college, the Army
Even war

It's nice to be experiencing
All sorts of things
For the first time

Even the poignancy
Of separation
Of loss
Real loss

It's, all of it, life
Real life

THE LEAVES

4:00 pm, Monday
November 10, 2014

I'm waiting
For the leaves to fall
From the peach tree

It has to get cold enough
For all the leaves to fall

It has to get cold enough
This winter
And the trees get
Really dormant

We may get fruit
Next year

Unlike this year

Nothing

No fruit

It just hadn't
Gotten cold enough
Last year

THE REALM

12:48 pm, Tuesday
November 11, 2014

You know
It's funny

No, not funny
It's glorious, really
Fantastic
Beyond belief

To live
For the moment
Or longer

In the realm
Of the spirit
All sorts of things
Inhabit there-in

Meditation
Prayer
Music
Especially music
Tchaikovsky's Fifth, . . . at this moment

SWEET MEMORIES

5:05 pm, Wednesday
November 13, 2014

Some years ago
When I was a member
Of the St. Genevieve's
Men's choir

Forty or fifty strong

We would give a concert
On occasion

Along with the boys choir
Forty or fifty strong

And seated in front of
The congregation
In the front row

I sat with Sal Milone
On my left
And Jerry Vuoso
On my right

And I would speak Sicilian
With Sal, a Sicilian,
And Neapolitan
With Jerry, a Neapolitan
Sotto voce

Sweet memories

YOUR OWN INSPIRATION

6:50 pm, Friday
December 5, 2014

You have a fine brain
But
To no avail
Don't you think
If it's not used
Its value
Is compromised,
As they say

Take important issues
Important decisions

Or if an admittedly
Useful insight
A valuable suggestion
Is made

To ask for details
For its implementation
Is to miss the point

Your own brain
Your own inspiration
Is called for
Not someone else's

THE C.I.A.

9:50 am, Wednesday
December 10, 2014

The C.I.A.
The Central Intelligence Agency
Is currently under fire
Accused of torturing
Prisoners
Beyond reasonable limits

Some
Or most critics
Say that the country
Does not stand for
Such things

Some say that
Our ideals
Represent "who we are"
Despite evidence to
The contrary

It's obvious
That both our
Torturing ways
And our frequently held
Ideals
Reveal who we are

HOW COULD YOU?

12:27 pm, Wednesday
December 10, 2014

How could you
Give up so much
Of yourself?

How could you surrender
So much
Your everything

For money

And the bargain made
What's left?
What's left of yourself?

Where did you learn this?
Who taught you?

You have my best wishes
That you will manage

And my love
And concern

NEVER BORING

3:35 pm, Friday
December 12, 2014
Our Lady of Guadalupe

Looking out the windows
Just now
I see a cloud formation
That's new

It was raining
Just now
And that may account
For the different shapes
And shades

I don't know much
About clouds
I couldn't name them
Their types

But they are fascinating
They seem
Always
To be different

Beautiful
Never boring

PREVIOUS BOOKS BY THE AUTHOR

Unlike the Vikings

Casta Diva

GrandMa and the Miracles

The Bird and the Squirrel

Rosalie Was All Night Without the Light

Chocolate and Cigarettes

RIVERSHORE BOOKS

Website:
www.rivershorebooks.com

Blog:
blog.rivershorebooks.com

Facebook:
www.facebook.com/rivershore.books

Twitter:
www.twitter.com/rivershorebooks

Email:
Jansina@rivershorebooks.com

The front cover is a scene in New York state in 1996.

www.ingramcontent.com/pod-product-compliance
Lightning Source LLC
Chambersburg PA
CBHW031519040426
42445CB00009B/312